AF220165

Notizbuch für Musiker

Notizbuch mit 5 mm Linien

Und lustigen Musiker-Katzen

Kurt Heppke

Bibliografische Information der Deutschen Nationalbibliothek:
Die Deutsche Nationalbibliothek verzeichnet diese Publikation in der Deutschen Nationalbibliografie; detaillierte bibliografische Daten sind im Internet über http://dnb.dnb.de abrufbar.

Herstellung und Verlag: BoD – Books on Demand, Norderstedt

ISBN: 978-3-7562-0905-7

DIESES BUCH GEHÖRT

Wow~

Get moody.....

Join me?

Music is served

Get high together

Follow me?

Let's groove

Can't resist...

Let's jazz !

Relax

It's your tempo~

Swing, girls swing!

You take the lead

Join me !

Hey, it's your tune!

Play it again, Sam~

enjoy...

Make it happen ~

Stay cool!

Have fun !

Swinging in the rain

Join me?

Leave me along

Bling!

Stay focus~

Tired?

Good day!

Welcome!

"Last call"

You coming?

Preparing....

My love....

Let me find my feet

Woops!

Be cool~

Go!!!

Mehr von mir können Sie hier finden:
https://www.kurtheppke.com/

Mehr von mir können Sie hier finden:
https://www.kurtheppke.com/